GIVE ME JESUS

A Collection of Thoughts, Prayers, and Stories

compiled by
Claire Jordan Mohan

Illustrations
Jane Robbins

YOUNG SPARROW PRESS
P.O. Box 265 • Worcester, PA 19490
(215) 364-1945
(215) 997-0791

Mohan, Claire Jordan
    Give Me Jesus, A Collection of Thoughts, Prayers and Stories

© Copyright 1998
Young Sparrow Press, Box 265, Worcester, PA 19490, (215) 364-1945, (215) 997-0791.
All rights reserved.
Printed in the United States of America.
First Printing.
Cover art by Jane Robbins.
All Scripture Quotations are from The Way, The Catholic Living Bible, Tynedale House Publishers, Inc., Wheaton, Illinois 60189 or
The Jerusalem Bible, Readers Edition, Doubleday & Co., Inc., Garden City, NY

ISBN #0-9621500-4-5 $7.95 paperback

To all children — everywhere.

"Suffer the children to come unto Me and forbid them not for of such is the Kingdom of Heaven."
Luke 10:4

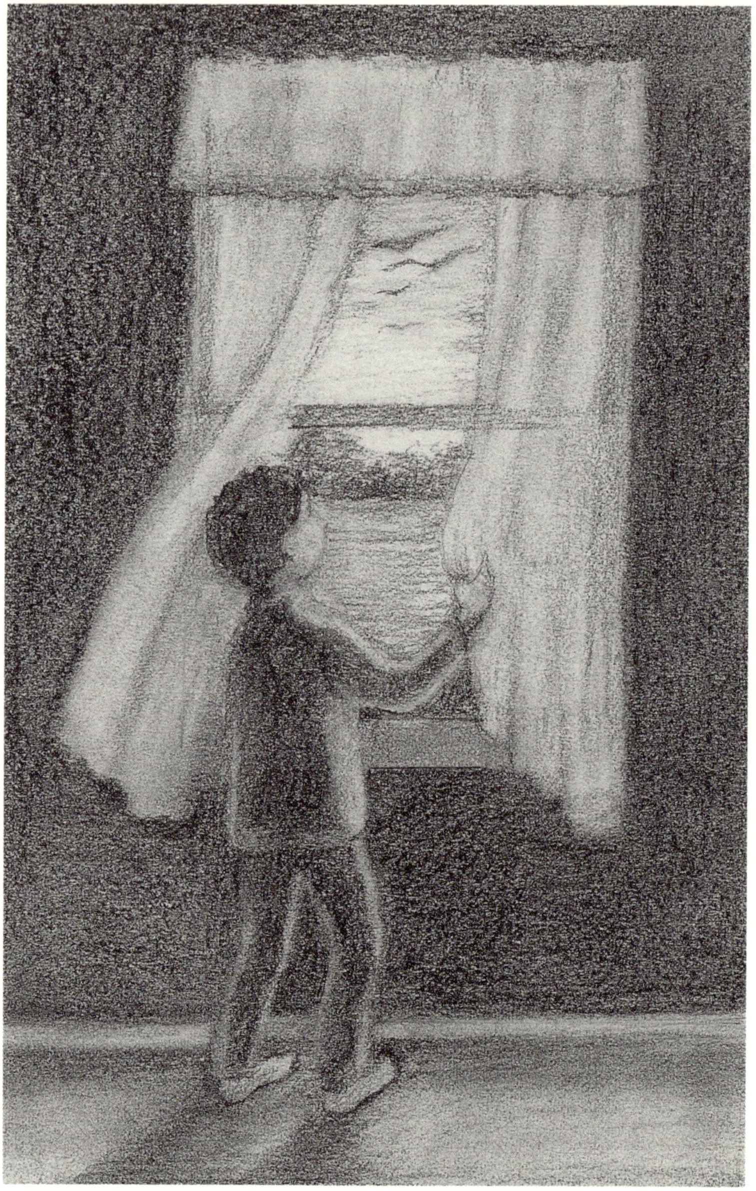

Give Me Jesus

Dear Reader,

Prayer is the lifting of the mind and heart to God. You can pray all day as you whisper your thoughts to Him and offer your actions, too. You may have conversations with Him at any time. You need not be on your knees. He is always tuned in to His children. Listen! You may hear His voice in your quiet moments. Sit in your room and wait for the soft whisper of God's love. Prayer is an important gift. It is our heart expressing our innermost self to Him.

Many people have shared their favorite prayers and stories to give you this book. Some of them are listed here:

> Sister Mary Campion S.S.J., Thomas Check Sr., Robert Delaney, Dolores Esmond, Claire Fitzgerald, Nancy Fogarty, Patricia Gallagher, Helen Galyen, Mary Ann Goldy, Eleanor Hentschel, Joann Hinkle, Anne Jordan, James G. Jordan Sr., Nancy Keller, Bessie Landis, Sister Leonilla S.S.J., Lorraine Liska, Helen McCracken, Claire Mohan, Mary Mohan, Robert Mohan, Ceil Moore, Lois Morris, Sister Patricia Murray S.N.D., Mary Musser, Maria Schneider, Mary Schratz, Clare Jordan-Schuster, Linda Shrake, Cassie Sieminski, Mary Stevens, Florence Stewart, Susannah Hart Thomer, Florence Wanner, and Susannah Kirk Zumbrotch.

We hope that this little book will bring joy to your life as you search its pages and find the words that have meaning to you.

contents

1
...in the morning
when I rise 9

2
...may I turn to Mary
when I pray 18

3
...as I travel
on life's way 21

4
...for my choices
along the way 31

5
...in my troubles
and my fears 39

6
...in the darkness
of the night 49

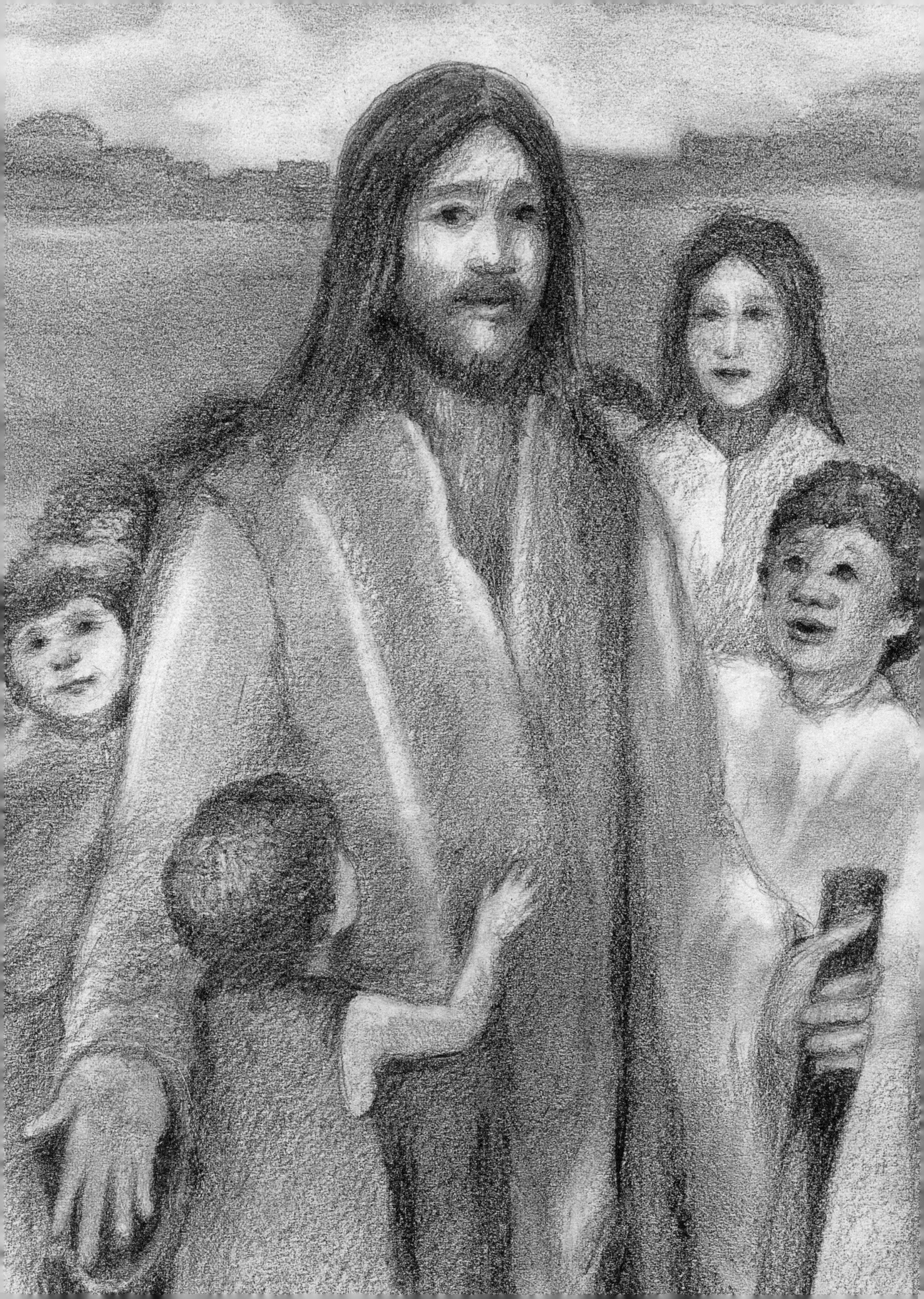

GIVE ME JESUS

In the morning when I rise, in the morning when I rise,
In the morning when I rise, give me Jesus.
Give me Jesus, give me Jesus.
You may have all this world, give me Jesus.

Dark midnight was my cry, dark midnight was my cry,
Dark midnight was my cry, give me Jesus.
Give me Jesus, give me Jesus.
You may have all this world, give me Jesus.

Just about the break of day, give me Jesus,
Just about the break of day, give me Jesus.
Give me Jesus, give me Jesus.
You may have all this world, give me Jesus.

O, when I come to die, O when I come to die,
O, when I come to die, give me Jesus.
Give me Jesus, give me Jesus.
You may have all this world, give me Jesus.

African-American

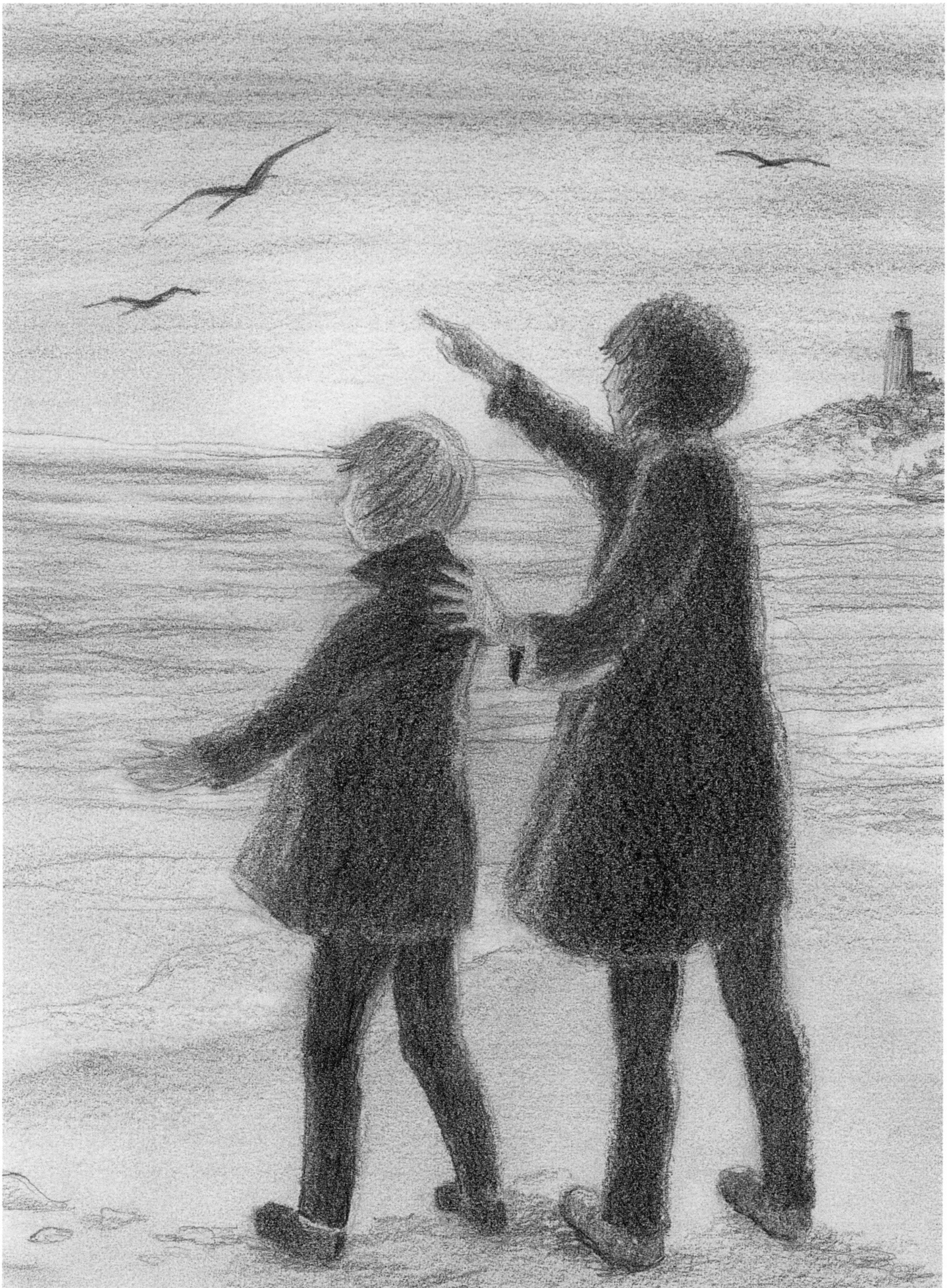

In the morning when I rise...
Give me Jesus

This day is mine, to mar to make.
God keep me strong and true.
Let me no erring by-paths take,
No doubtful actions do.

My God, I offer you this day,
   all I think or do or say.

Thank you, dear Jesus, for keeping us safe through the night.
Please keep us good and safe through the day.
I offer my day to you.

Little King, so sweet and kind
I kneel each morn to pray,
And tell you that I love you
In my sweet and childlike way.

Enjoy the blessings of this day, if God sends them; and the evils of it, bear patiently and sweetly; for this day only is ours; we are dead to yesterday, and we are not yet born to the morrow.

There is no spot where God is not.

Teach Me, My Lord

Teach me, my Lord, to be sweet and gentle in all the events of life. In my disappointments, in the thoughtlessness of others; in the insincerity of those I trusted; in the untruthfulness of those in whom I relied.

Let me put myself aside to think of the happiness of others, to hide my little pains and heartaches so that I will be the only one to suffer from them.

Teach me to profit by the suffering that comes across my path.

Let me use it that it may mellow me, not harden nor embitter me; that it may make me patient, not irritable; that it may make me broad in my forgiveness, not narrow, haughty, and overbearing.

May no one be less good for having come within my influence. No one less pure, less true, less kind, less noble for having been a fellow traveler in our journey towards Eternal Life.

As I make my rounds from one distraction to another, let me whisper from time to time a word of love to Thee. May my life be lived in the supernatural, full of power for good and strong in its purpose of sanctity.

If I can do some good today,
If I can serve along life's way,
If I can something helpful say,
Lord show me how.

If I can right a human wrong,
If I can help to make one strong,
If I can cheer with smile or song,
Lord, show me how.

If I can aid one in distress,
If I can make a burden less,
If I can spread more happiness,
Lord, show me how.

Don't say you don't have enough time. You have exactly the same number of hours per day that were given to Helen Keller, Louis Pasteur, Michelangelo, Mother Teresa, Leonardo da Vinci, Thomas Jefferson, Thomas Edison, and Albert Einstein.

Czechoslovakian Morning Prayer

My Jesus, be on my mind, my lips, and in my heart. I offer up everything I may think, say, and do, every step that I take, every breath that I make, all my labors, all my suffering of this day for my soul's salvation and Your adoration. Amen.

Let the beauty of Jesus be seen in me—
All His wonderful passion and purity.
Oh, thou Spirit Divine, all my nature refine
Till the beauty of Jesus be seen in me.

Angel of God, my guardian dear,
Through whom God's love
Commits me here.
Ever this day, be at my side—
To light, to guard, to rule, to guide.

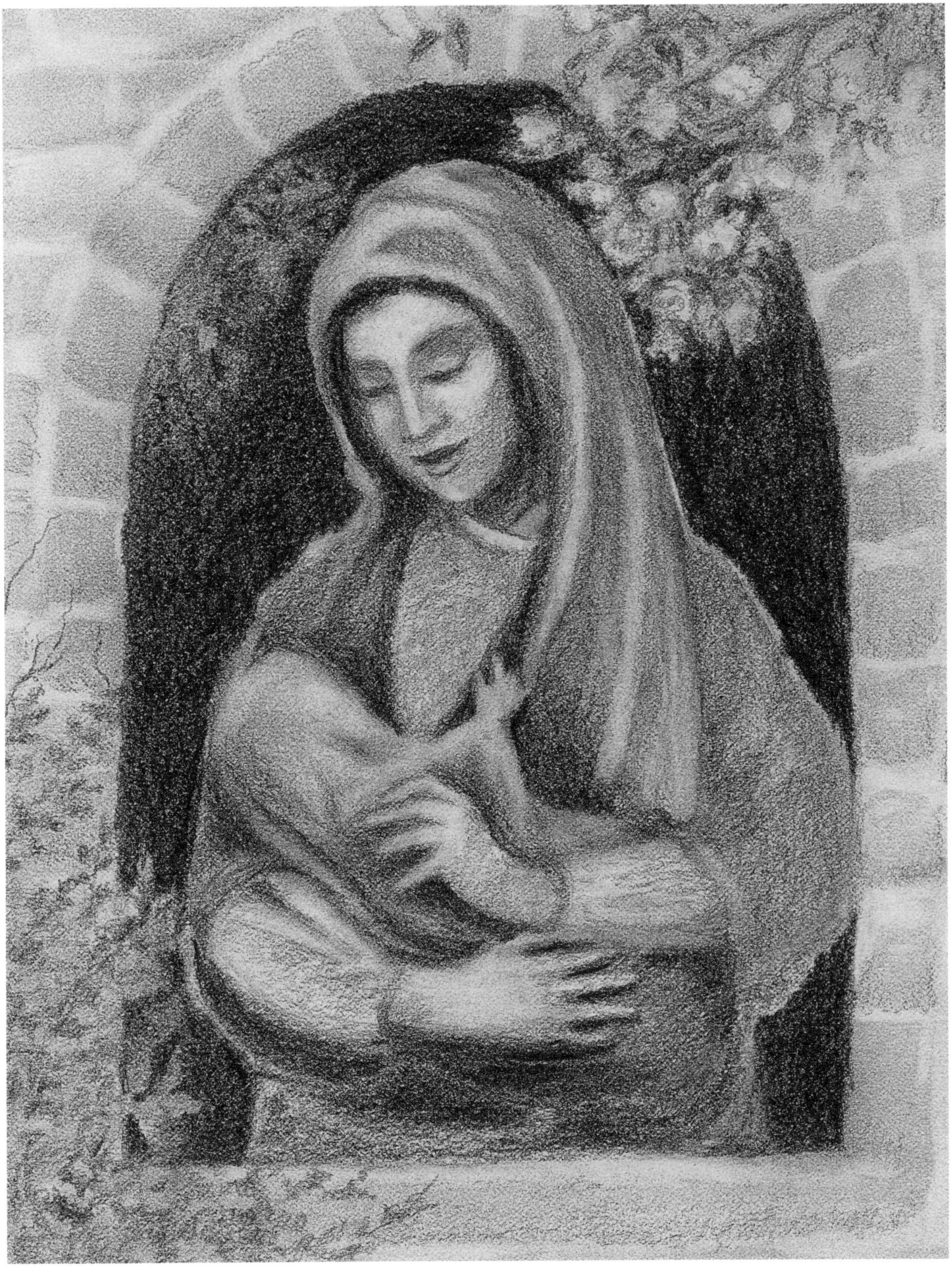

*All throughout the blessed day...
May I turn to Mary when I pray*

My Rosary Beads

I have a pair of rosary beads,
As plain as plain can be,
And only God in Heaven knows
How dear they are to me.

I have them always with me,
At every step I take,
At evening when I slumber,
At morning when I wake.

And when the time approaches
That I shall have to die,
I hope my little rosary beads
Will close beside me lie.

And that the holy name of Jesus
May be the last I say,
And kissing my dear rosary beads,
My soul shall pass away.

Hail Mary

Hail Mary, full of grace, the Lord is with thee. Blessed art thou amongst women, and blessed is the fruit of thy womb, Jesus. Holy Mary, Mother of God, pray for us sinners, now and at the hour of our death. Amen.

The angel Gabriel was sent by God to a town in Galilee called Nazareth to a virgin betrothed to a man named Joseph, of the House of David; and the virgin's name was Mary. He went in and said to her, "Rejoice, so highly favored! The Lord is with you." She was deeply disturbed by these words and asked herself what this greeting could mean, but the angel said to her, "Mary, do not be afraid; you have won God's favor. Listen! You are to conceive and bear a son, and you must name him Jesus. He will be great and will be called Son of the Most High. The Lord God will give him the throne of his ancestor David; he will rule over the House of Jacob forever and his reign will have no end." Mary said to the angel, "But how can this come about, since I am a virgin?" "The Holy Spirit will come upon you," the angel answered, "and the power of the Most High will cover you with its shadow. And so the child will be holy and will be called Son of God."

Luke 1:26-38

Mary set out at that time and went as quickly as she could to a town in the hill country of Judah. She went into Zechariah's house and greeted her cousin Elizabeth. Now as soon as Elizabeth heard Mary's greeting, the child leaped in her womb and Elizabeth was filled with the Holy Spirit. She gave a loud cry and said, "Of all women you are the most blessed, and blessed is the fruit of your womb."

Luke 1:39-42

Give Me Jesus

Mary, my mother, I place myself under thy mantle.
There I wish to live and die. Keep me from sin and bless me.

Dear Blessed Mother, be forever at my side.

Immaculate Mother of God, we choose thee to be the lady of this house. Guard it from fire, water, enemies, burglars, and disease. Protect its inmates, sweet Mary. Watch over their going out and their coming in. Pray that all may live in God's service and depart this life in His grace. Amen.

Mary, place thy Jesus
Within my cradled heart.
Rock it soft with thy dear hands
Lest He should thence depart.
But should He find it cold and strange
In this poor heart of mine,
Tell Him I am just a child
And all I have is thine.

O Mary, my Mother and My Lady, I offer You my soul, my body, my life and my death, and all that will follow it. I place everything in your hands. O my Mother, cover my soul with your virginal mantle and grant me the grace of purity of heart, soul, and body.

Sister Faustina

Lovely Lady dressed in Blue
Teach me how to pray!
God was just your little Boy,
Tell me what to say!
Did you lift Him up, sometimes,
Gently on your knee?
Did you sing to Him the way
Mother does to me?
Did you hold His hand at night?
Did you ever try
Telling stories of the world?
O! And did he cry?
Do you really think He cares
If I tell Him things—
Little things that happen?
And
Do the angels' wings
Make a noise?
And can He hear
Me if I speak low?
Does He understand me now?
Tell me—for you know.
Lovely Lady dressed in blue,
Teach me how to pray!
God was just your little Boy,
And you know the way.

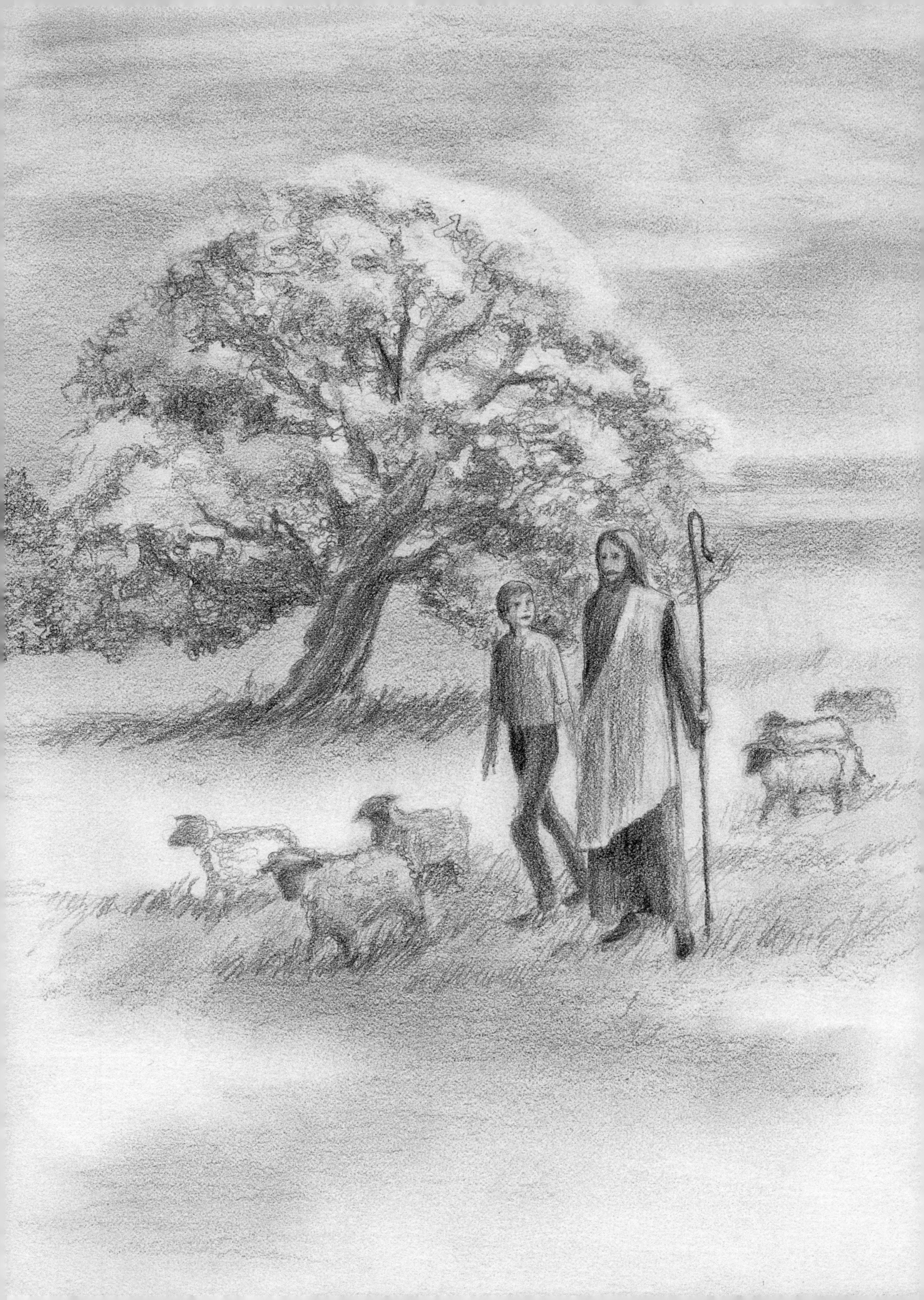

As I travel on life's way...
Give me Jesus

Give Me Jesus

God is great
God is good.
Let us thank Him for our food.
By His hand we all are fed.
Give us, Lord, our daily bread.

---

*Come, Lord Jesus, our Guest to be
And bless these gifts bestowed by Thee.*

Thank you for the world so sweet,
Thank you for the food we eat,
Thank you for the birds that sing.
Thank you, God, for everything.

Heavenly Father
We thank Thee for our food
And we ask Thee to bless it
For Your honor and for our good,
So we can serve you better. Amen.

The Lord is my light and my salvation; He protects me from danger—whom shall I fear? When evil men come to destroy me, they will stumble and fall! Yea, though a mighty army marches against me, my heart shall know no fear! I am confident that God will save me.

Psalm 27:1-3

The Lord is my Shepherd. I have everything I need! He lets me rest in the meadow grass and leads me beside the quiet streams. He gives me new strength. He helps me do what honors him most. Even when walking through the dark valley of death, I will not be afraid, for You are close beside me, guarding, guiding all the way. You provide delicious food for me in the presence of my enemies. You have welcomed me as Your guest; blessings overflow! Your goodness and unfailing kindness shall be with me all of my life, and afterwards I will live with You forever in Your home.

Psalm 23

Samuel was sleeping in the temple of the Lord where the Ark of God was. The Lord called to Samuel, who answered, "Here I am." He ran to Eli and said, "Here I am. You called me." "I did not call you," Eli said. "Go back to sleep." So he went back to sleep. Again the Lord called Samuel, who rose and went to Eli. "Here I am," he said. "You called me." But he answered, "I did not call you, my son. Go back to sleep." At that time Samuel was not familiar with the Lord, because the Lord had not revealed anything to him as yet. The Lord called Samuel again, for the third time. Getting up and going to Eli, he said, "Here I am. You called me." Then Eli understood that the Lord was calling the youth. So he said to Samuel, "Go to sleep and if you are called, reply, 'Speak, Lord, for your servant is listening.'" When Samuel went to sleep in his place, the Lord came and revealed his presence, calling out as before, "Samuel, Samuel!" Samuel answered, "Speak, for your servant is listening."

Samuel grew up, and the Lord was with him, not permitting any word of his to be without effect.

1 Samuel 3:3-10, 19

The Maxims of St. Theresa of Avila

Let nothing trouble you,
Let nothing affright you,
All things pass away.
God never changes.
Patience obtains everything.
God alone suffices.

Give what you have. To someone, it may be better than you dare to think.
Henry Wadsworth Longfellow

As you wander on through life,
Whatever be your goal,
Keep your eye upon the donut
And not upon the hole!

Kindness — a language which the dumb can speak,
and the deaf understand.
Christian Bivee

The little drops of rain
The little grains of sand
Make the mighty ocean
And the pleasant land.

The little deeds of kindness,
The little words of love
Make this life on Eden
Like the Heaven above.

Love your enemies, do good to those who hate you, bless those who curse you, pray for those who treat you badly. Treat others as you would like them to treat you.

Luke 6:27-28, 31

You must love the Lord your God with all your heart, with all your soul, with all your strength, and with all your mind, and your neighbor as yourself. Do this and life is yours.

Luke 10:27-28

Just saying that "I love you"
doesn't mean a thing at all,
For loving words fly like the birds
When they hear winter's call.

Love is a thing that proves itself
a thousand times a day,
In the simple little things you do
and the little things you say.

Love is a thing called sacrifice,
a tonic when you're blue.
Love is the joy of doing things
for someone dear to you.

Oh Jesus, make Yourself to me,
A living bright reality.
More precious to faith's vision keen
Than any outward object seen.
More dear, more intimately nigh
Than even the sweetest earthly tie.

Give Me Jesus

Our Father, who art in Heaven
Hallowed be Thy name.
Thy kingdom come, thy will be done
On earth as it is in Heaven.
Give us this day our daily bread
And forgive us our trespasses
As we forgive those
Who trespass against us.
And lead us not into temptation
But deliver us from evil. Amen.

Once when Jesus had been out praying, one of his disciples came to him as he finished and said, "Lord, teach us to pray, just as John taught his disciples."

And this is the prayer he taught them:

> "Father, may your name be held holy,
> Your kingdom come;
> Give us each day our daily bread,
> and forgive us our sins,
> for we ourselves forgive each one who is
> in debt to us. And do not put us to the test."

Then teaching them more about prayer, he used this illustration: "Suppose you went to a friend's house at midnight, wanting to borrow three loaves of bread. You would shout up to him, 'A friend of mine has just arrived for a visit and I've nothing to give him to eat.' He would call down from his bedroom. 'Please don't ask me to get up. The door is locked for the night and we are all in bed. I just can't help you this time.'

"But I'll tell you this—though he won't do it as a friend, if you keep knocking long enough, he will get up and give you everything you want—just because of your persistence. And so it is with prayer—keep on asking and you will keep on getting; keep on looking and you will keep on finding; knock and the door will be opened. Everyone who asks, receives; all who seek, find; and the door is opened to everyone who knocks."

Luke 11:1-10

I expect to pass through this world but once. Any good, therefore, that I can do or any kindness that I can show to my fellow creatures, let me not defer nor neglect it, for I shall not pass this way again.

When I was in fifth grade I learned a worthwhile lesson about life. It taught me to look at any given situation from another angle to really understand the circumstances. Back then, I thought I was really something and part of the "in crowd" at school.

I remember coming home from school one day and complaining to my mother about a boy in my class who had been following me around, trying to sit next to me and generally making a pest of himself. He definitely had a crush on me, but I was only interested in my own selective group of friends. He was a shy, introverted ten-year-old who had a lisp and was, what the kids today would call, "a nerd". "I can't get rid of him," I told my mother.

Instead of telling me what a stuck-up kid I was, my mother turned the whole situation around by presenting the positive side. She took my face and looked right into my eyes and told me that I must be a very, very special person to this boy. After all, he had chosen me over everybody else to share his most precious gift, and that was his love. "You are such a lucky person because this gift is the most cherished anyone could offer you," she said. "You should receive it as graciously as it was given." She taught me not only to be receptive to love, but to give it as honestly and openly as that little boy had.

Susannah Hart Thomer

If I can stop one heart from breaking
I shall not live in vain.
If I can ease one life that's aching,
Or cool one pain,
Or help one fainting robin
Upon his nest again,
I shall not live in vain.

It is better to light one candle than to curse the darkness.
Motto of Christopher Society

No act of kindness, no matter how small is ever forgotten.

Be kind, honest and true;
For you never know when your words or actions
May come back to you.

Think carefully before speaking. Just as toothpaste squeezed from the tube cannot be put back in — no matter how little — the wrong words thoughtlessly spoken can create a harmful mess.

Never lose an opportunity of seeing anything that is beautiful,
for beauty is God's handwriting — a wayside sacrament.
Ralph Waldo Emerson

Wise is the child who knows what to say, but when not to say it.

Love is always patient and kind; it is never jealous; love is never boastful or conceited; it is never rude or selfish; it does not take offense, and is not resentful. Love takes no pleasure in other people's sins but delights in the truth; it is always ready to excuse, to trust, to hope, and to endure whatever comes. In short, there are three things that last: faith, hope, and love, and the greatest of these is love.
I Corinthians 13:4-7, 13

Give Me Jesus

Life is mostly froth and bubbles
Two things stand like stone
Kindness in another's trouble
Courage in one's own.
Adam Lindsay Gordon

We must do small things for one another with great love.
Mother Teresa

Hold fast to dreams
For if dreams die
Life is a broken-winged bird
That cannot fly.

Hold fast to dreams
For when dreams go
Life is a barren field
Frozen with snow.
Langston Hughes

"Where shall I work today, dear Lord?"
And my love flowed warm and free.
He answered and said, "See that little place?
Tend that place for Me."
I answered and said, "Oh no, not there!
No one would ever see.
No matter how well my work was done,
Not that little place for me!"
His voice, when He spoke, was soft and kind,
He answered me tenderly,
"Little one, search that heart of thine,
Are you working for them...or Me?
Nazareth was a little place...so was Galilee."

Give Me Jesus

IXOYE

I AM ONE

I am only one,

But still I am one

I cannot do everything,

But I can still do something;

And because I cannot do everything

I will not refuse to do the

something that I can do.

Edward Everett Hale

High Flight

(Written by a 19-year-old American volunteer with the Royal Canadian Air Force, who was killed in action December 11, 1941)

Oh, I have slipped the surly bonds of earth,
And danced the skies on laughter-silvered wings;
Sunward I've climbed and joined the tumbling mirth
Of sun-split clouds — and done a hundred things
You have not dreamed of — wheeled and soared and swung
High in the sunlit silence. Hov'ring there,
I've chased the shouting wind along and flung
My eager craft through footless halls of air.
Up, up the long, delirious, burning blue
I've topped the wind-swept heights with easy grace,
Where never lark, or even eagle flew;
And, while with silent, lifting mind I've trod
The high untrespassed sanctity of space,
Put out my hand, and touched the face of God.
John Gillespie Magee, Jr.

Broken Dreams

As children bring their broken toys
With tears for us to mend,
I brought my broken dreams to God
Because He was my Friend.

But then instead of leaving Him
In peace to work alone,
I hung around and tried to help
With ways that were my own.

At last I snatched them back and cried,
"How can You be so slow—"
"My child," He said, "what could I do?
You never did let go."

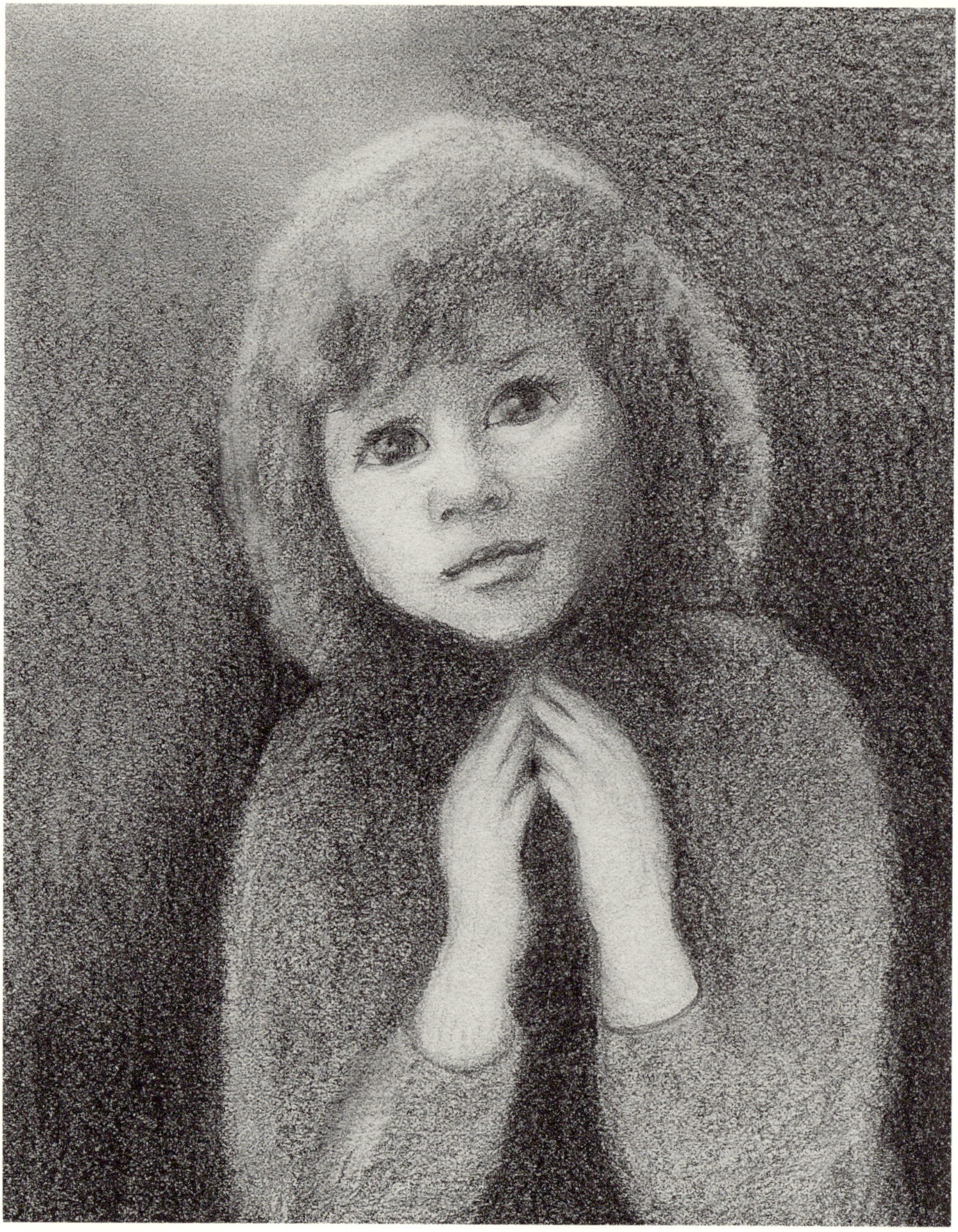

For my choices along the way...
Give me Jesus

The Wisdom of the Great Master

When I was about eight years old I was given a homework assignment in school to translate the meaning of the famous Shakespeare quote, "What's in a name, a rose by any other name would smell as sweet."

At the time I did not realize how hard this assignment actually was for an eight year old, but it was to be a significant episode in the development of my self-esteem and beliefs about life.

That night, when I pulled out my book and read the quote, I thought about its meaning. For a long time I pondered over it, but I remained perplexed. I looked at each word. I understood every one of them. Somehow the combination of these sixteen words made them all foreign. After what seemed like hours, I headed off to the Great Master problem-solver himself, DAD. I knew he would give me some words of wisdom that would make this problem a snap.

Well, needless to say, I was going to learn that life was not that easy. The only aid dad would afford me was, "Just THINK about it, Clare." "What?! That's it!"

I remember at the time thinking, "What do you think I have been doing?" So back to the big, white formica kitchen table went a disgruntled Clare. I will never forget the feeling of frustration I felt sitting there at the table kicking the post with my foot while enunciating every word over and over. "What, is, in, a, name," sighing deeply. "A, rose, by, any, other, name, would, smell, as, sweet," I would scowl, getting angrier and angrier at the supposed Great Master, fixer of all childhood problems.

I remember thinking it was impossible and wanting to give up. Although I was almost in tears, there was something inside me that didn't let me. Suddenly, I felt something. Even though at this point I was physically and mentally drained, I mustered up the energy to pay attention to what was happening inside my brain. The whole world around me stopped as I refocused my attention on the words. Next, I had a surge of thoughts and ideas. Then I had an answer which only moments before had seemed impossible. I dashed into the living room and proclaimed my explanation to my dad. Never before had I felt so proud and independent as I explained to him that even though God creates all of the things we have in life, we, as human beings, give them names. I knew he was proud of me for my patience and determination, but that didn't matter, I was!

Years later as I reflect on that night when I asked the Great Master for his wisdom, I have come to believe that what he was telling me was the gifts of knowledge and understanding are received through the belief in oneself!

Clare Jordan-Schuster

Dear God,
give us strength and grace to persevere.

The little troubles and worries of life, so many of which we meet, may be stumbling blocks in our way, or we may make them stepping stones on the stairs to Heaven.

When things go wrong, as they sometimes will, when the road you're traveling seems all uphill, when the funds are low and the debts are high, when you want to smile, but you have to sigh, when care is pressing you down a bit, rest if you want — but don't you quit.

Life is queer with its twists and turns, as every one of us sometimes learns, and many a failure turns about, when he might have won had he stuck it out. Don't give up though the pace seems slow. You may succeed with another blow.

Success is failure turned inside out, the silver tint of the clouds of doubt, and you never can tell how close you are. It may be near when it seems so far. So stick to the fight when you're hardest hit. It's when things seem worse that you must not quit!

Do your best and God will do the rest.

One day, Jesus got into a boat with his disciples and said to them, "Let us cross over to the other side of the lake." So they put to sea, and as they sailed he fell asleep. When a squall came down on the lake, the boat started taking in water and they found themselves in danger. So they went to rouse him saying, "Master, Master! We are going down!" Then he woke up and rebuked the wind and the rough water; and they subsided and it was calm again. He said to them, "Where is your faith?" They were awestruck and astonished and said to one another, "Who can this be, that gives orders even to winds and waves and they obey him?"

Luke 8:22-25

You're beaten to earth
Oh, well, what's that?
Be proud of your blackened eye.
It's not the fact that you're licked that counts.
It's how you were licked, and why.

In a race everyone runs, but only one person gets first prize. So run your race to win. To win the contest you must deny yourselves many things that would keep you from doing your best. An athlete goes to all this trouble just to win a blue ribbon or a silver cup, but we do it for a heavenly reward that never disappears. So I run straight to the goal with purpose in every step. I fight to win. I'm not just shadow-boxing or playing around. Like an athlete, I punish my body, treating it roughly, training it to do what it should, not what it wants to. Otherwise I fear that after enlisting others for the race, I myself might be declared unfit and ordered to stand aside.

I Corinthians 9:24-27

If at first you don't succeed, never stop for crying.
All that's good or great is done just by patient trying.

If by easy work you beat, who the more will prize you?
Getting victory from defeat, that's the test that tries you.

As you go through the steps of life,
 Whatever it be — happiness or strife,
 Remember you always have a friend from above.
He will never forsake you
Only give you His love.

Continue to love each other like brothers, and remember always to welcome strangers, for by doing this, some people have entertained angels without knowing it.

Hebrews 13:1-2

The Chime of My Life

The love of God for small children is well documented. He tells us that we must become like small children in order to enter Heaven. I had an experience as an altar boy when I needed every reassurance of His love for the youth.

It was to be my big moment! I had finally reached age nine, and I was to serve my first Mass. How proud I was! My mother lovingly inspected my clothes, tidied my hair, shined my shoes and I was off to begin my new career!

As I entered the sacristy, the priest smiled at me and welcomed me to the brotherhood of the service of God. I donned my cassock with pride, looking in the mirror to be sure everything was just perfect. I had a few butterflies in my stomach, but I was filled with the burning zeal of religious service, and I felt totally in control.

Finally, the hour struck, and I proudly walked out onto the altar. I sneaked a peek to see how many people were in attendance, and I recall being very happy to see so many there to watch my debut.

Everything, at first, went swimmingly. I remembered every instruction I had been given, and I went through my routine without missing a cue. After the sermon, and when time for the Consecration arrived, I felt like a pro. In those days we had either bells or chimes to be rung. It was the high point of the Mass for the server. At our church, we had chimes which meant I had an even larger part to play as there were five notes to be struck.

At last, my big moment arrived. As the priest raised the Host, I very magnificently struck the first note. The sound was beautiful and I was filled with joy! I raised the mallet and struck the second note with ever more passion. Ah, how lovely! The third note, I struck with even more fervor. At that point, to my abject horror, the rubber ball on the end of the mallet popped off and bounced across the floor. I was frozen in horror. I watched anxiously to see where it went, jumped to my feet and scurried after it.

I finally located it and returned to my position with my face red and my head bowed in shame. Finally, I looked at the priest, hoping he would not be staring at me with disdain. To my relief, he looked at me, smiled and winked. Suddenly, it was all okay. I realized that Our Lord, too, must have been smiling at me.

If this experience taught me anything, it was that we should not take ourselves too seriously. Our Loving Father has a terrific sense of humor. After all, He did make us!

Bob Delaney

Just for a Minute

I remember when I was only four,
Mother would bring me 'round to the store,
And just outside of the church she'd stand,
And "Come in," she'd say, reaching down for my hand
    "Just for a minute."

And then when I started going to school,
She'd bring me down every day as a rule,
But first the steps to the church we'd climb,
And she'd say, "We'll go in, you've always got time,
    Just for a minute."

Then I got real big, I mean seven years old,
And I went by myself, but was always told,
"When you're passing the church, don't forget to call
And tell Our Lord about lessons and all,
    Just for a minute."

Sometimes I run most of the way,
Or meet some guys and we stop to play,
But I manage to squeeze out time enough
To make the church where I pant and puff,
    Just for a minute.

And now it's sort of a habit I've got,
In the evening, coming from Casey's lot
Though it takes me out of my way a bit,
To slip into church with my hat and mitt,
    Just for a minute.

But sometimes I see the other fellow
Standing around and I just go yellow.
I pass by the door, but a Voice within
Seems to say, real sad, "So you wouldn't come in,
    Just for a minute."

There are things inside me, bad and good,
That nobody knows and nobody could,
Excepting Our Lord, and I like Him to know,
And He helps, when in for a visit I go,
    Just for a minute.

I know what happens when people die,
But I won't be scared, and I'll tell you why,
When Our Lord is judging my soul, I feel
He'll remember the times I went in to kneel,
    Just for a minute.

I am the light that God shines through
For He and I are one, not two.
So if I be relaxed and free
He will carry out His plan through me.

Be compassionate as your Father is compassionate.
Do not judge and you will not be judged yourselves;
do not condemn and you will not be condemned yourselves;
grant pardon and you will be pardoned.
Give and there will be gifts for you.

Luke 6:36-38

I am a princess
Though few might know.
In my quiet praying
God tells me so.

My heart is an altar
And all day long
I keep singing
A happy song.

There is a dream
In the heart of me.
I'll be a princess
For eternity.

Full lasting is the song, though he,
The singer, passes.

George Meredith

The Unknown Quantity

When the world was new and the early sun
    First shone upon sea and land,
When nothing had died and nothing had failed
    Of all that the Lord had planned;
The Lord looked down on His handiwork,
    On the beasts and the birds and the trees,
And He smiled as He said, "Behold, I will make
    A greater thing than these."

So He fashioned man, and He gave him life
    And power for his daily task,
But, "For aught that thou needest more," He said,
    "Thou shalt turn unto Me and ask."
And one more thing He put in the world,
    The greatest of all to be,
And He hid it deep in the soul of man, —
    The Unknown Quantity.

For He knew that the world would grow old and tired,
    And that man could not do his part
Unless he possessed that hidden strength
    To comfort his failing heart; —
The will to pray and the power to play
    That last and highest card,
So that, "What he asks shall be done," said the Lord,
    "Because he has prayed so hard."

And still the Lord of Hosts looks down
    On a world grown old with care,
And still He puts in the hearts of men
    That unknown gift of prayer.
And to those who pray with all their strength,
    Which is all that the best can do,
His promise stands as it always stood: —
    "Behold, I make all things new."

Ethel M. Dell

Give Me Jesus

Many, many years ago, in the early days of Christianity when the Church was young, the followers of Jesus were not accepted. They were pursued by the Romans and imprisoned or killed.
One day one of these early Christians was being chased by Roman soldiers. He was frightened and didn't know how to escape. As he ran, he noticed a cave. He dashed into the dark space and decided to hide there.
Almost immediately, a spider came along and quickly spun a web which covered the whole entrance. Then the wind blew dust onto it. Moments later, the Roman soldiers came by. They glanced at the cave and said, "No sense looking in there. That old spider web has been there for years", and they continued on their way. God used the spider to save the one who loved him.

Everybody can be great... because anybody can serve.
You don't have to have a college degree to serve.
You don't have to make your noun and verb agree to serve.
You only need a heart full of grace.
A soul generated by love.

Martin Luther King, Jr.

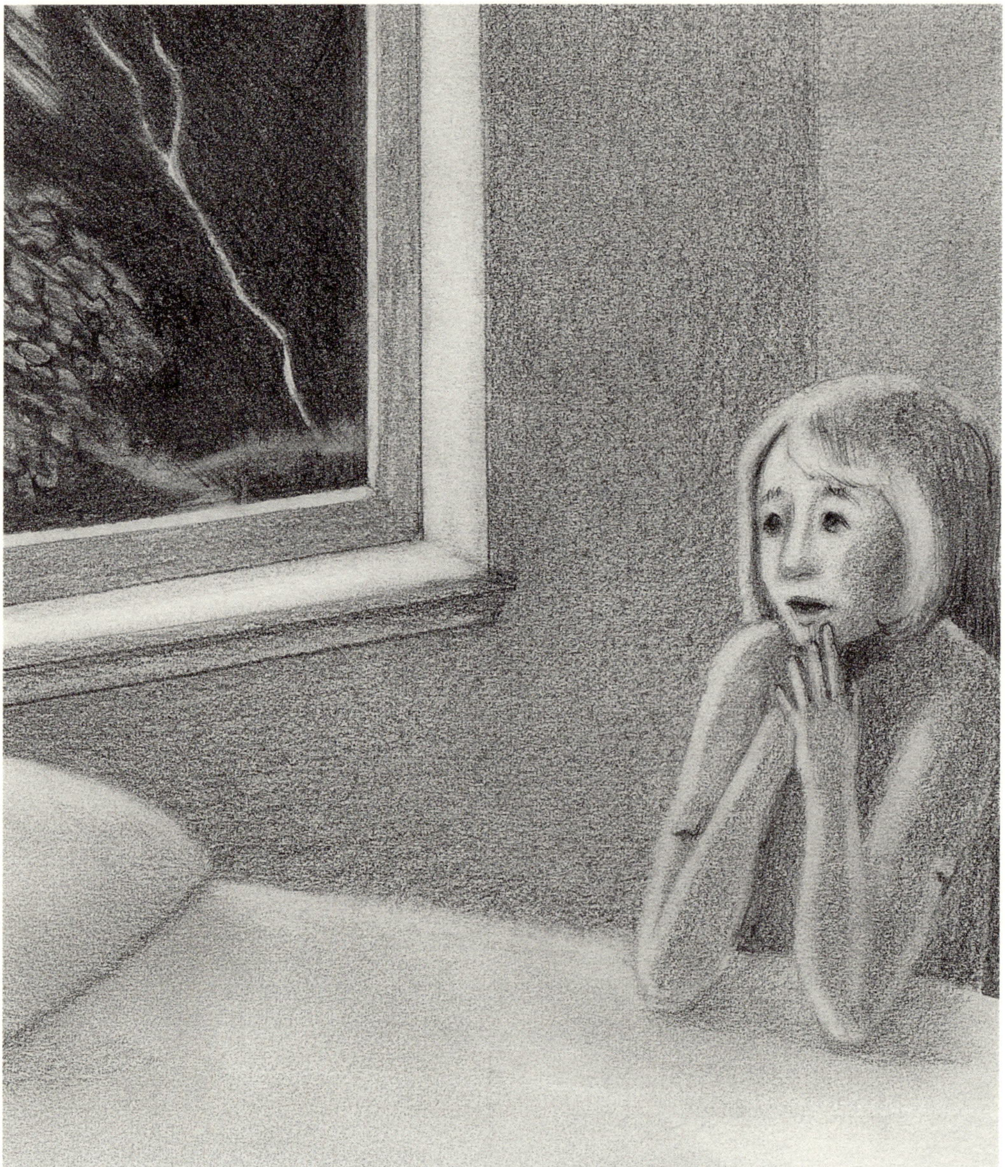

In my troubles and my fears...
Give me Jesus

The cross is tall, and I too small
To reach His hands or touch His feet,
But on the sand, His footprints I have found
And it is sweet to kiss the holy ground.

---

*Whatsoever you do to the least of my brothers,
that you do unto Me.
Matthew 25:31*

There was a lawyer who stood up to Jesus and said to him, "Master, what must I do to inherit eternal life?" He said to him, "What is written in the Law? What do you read there?" He replied, "You must love the Lord your God with all your heart, with all your soul, with all your strength, and with all your mind, and your neighbor as yourself." "You have answered right," said Jesus, "do this and life is yours."

But the man was anxious to justify himself and said to Jesus, "And who is my neighbor?" Jesus replied, "A man was once on his way down from Jerusalem to Jericho and fell into the hands of brigands; they took all he had, beat him and then made off, leaving him half dead. Now a priest happened to be traveling down the same road, but when he saw the man, he passed on the other side. In the same way a Levite who came to the place saw him and passed by on the other side. But a Samaritan saw him. He went up and bandaged his wounds, pouring oil and wine on them. He then lifted him on his own mount, carried him to the inn and looked after him. Next day, he took out two denarii and handed them to the innkeeper. 'Look after him,' he said, 'and on my way back I will make good any extra expense you have.' Which of these three, do you think, proved himself a neighbor to the man who fell into the brigand's hands?" "The one who took pity on him," he replied. Jesus said to him, "Go and do the same yourself."

Luke 10:30-37

What man among you with a hundred sheep, losing one, would not leave the ninety-nine in the wilderness and go after the missing one till he found it. And when he found it, would he not joyfully take it on his shoulders and then when he got home, call together his friends and neighbors? "Rejoice with me," he would say, "I have found my sheep that was lost." In the same way, I tell you, there will be rejoicing in heaven over one repentant sinner than over ninety-nine virtuous men who have no need of repentance."

Luke 15:4-7

Lo, I am with you always, even unto the end of the world.
Luke 28:20

I said to the man who stood at the gate of the year, "Give me a light that I may tread safely in the unknown. And he said, "Go out into the darkness and put thine hand into the hand of God. This will be to thee better than a light and safer than a known way."

M. Louise Harkins

He will put you in his angels' charge to guard you wherever you go.
Psalm 91:11

Always treat others as you would like them to treat you.
Matt 7:12

Whether you think you can or think you can't, you're right!
Henry Ford

Give Me Jesus

When I was six years old, I had a severe ear infection. In those days doctors did not have antibiotics to help them. There was no cure for the heavy drainage from my ear and the terrible pain. Finally, I was told I had to go to the hospital for a mastoidectomy—an operation on my ear.

My mother asked an Army Chaplain who was a friend of our family if he would come to visit me in the hospital. The nurses had prepared me for the surgery. Already they had shaved the hair from the right side of my head. It was late that night when the chaplain arrived. He prayed for me and then he blessed my ear with a relic of the True Cross.

The next morning I was taken to the operating room. The doctor and nurses were ready. Before he began surgery, the doctor examined my ear. He turned to my parents and asked, "What is this child doing here? There is nothing wrong with her ear!"

There was no sign of the mastoiditis! I was discharged after two more days and had no more problems with my ears.

And now a man named Jairus, a leader of a Jewish synagogue, came and fell at Jesus' feet and begged him to come home with him for his only child was dying, a little girl twelve years old. Jesus went with him, pushing through the crowds.

A messenger arrived from the Jairus' home with the news that the little girl was dead. "She's gone," he told her father, "there's no use troubling the Teacher now." But when Jesus heard what had happened, he said to the father, "Don't be afraid! Just trust me, and she'll be all right."

When they arrived at the house, Jesus wouldn't let anyone into the room except Peter, James, John, and the little girl's father and mother. The home was filled with mourning people, but he said, "Stop the weeping! She isn't dead; she is only asleep." This brought scoffing and laughter for they all knew she was dead.

Then he took her by the hand and called, "Get up, little girl!" And at that moment her life returned and she jumped up! "Give her something to eat!" he said. Her parents were overcome with happiness.

Luke 8:42, 49-54

> If your brother does something wrong, reprove him and,
> if he is sorry, forgive him. And if he wrongs you seven times a day...
> you must forgive him.
> *Luke 17:4*

A man had two sons. The younger one said to his father, "Father, let me have the share of the estate that would come to me." So the father divided the property between them. A few days later, the younger son got together everything he had and left for a distant country where he squandered his money.

When he had spent it all, that country experienced a severe famine, and he began to feel the pinch. So he hired himself out to one of the local inhabitants who put him on his farm to feed the pigs. And he would willingly have filled his belly with the husks the pigs were eating but no one offered him anything. Then he came to his senses and said, "How many of my father's paid servants have more food than they want, and here I am dying of hunger! I will leave this place and go to my father and say: 'Father, I have sinned against heaven and against you; I no longer deserve to be called your son; treat me as one of your paid servants.' " So he left the place and went back to his father.

While he was still a long way off, his father saw him and was moved with pity. He ran to the boy, clasped him in his arms and kissed him tenderly. Then his son said, "Father I have sinned against heaven and against you. I no longer deserve to be called your son." But the father said to his servants, "Quick! Bring out the best robe and put it on him; put a ring on his finger and sandals on his feet. Bring the calf we have been fattening, and kill it; we are going to have a feast because this son of mine was dead and has come back to life; he was lost and is found." And they began to celebrate.

Luke 15:11-32

The best thing to give your enemy is forgiveness;
to an opponent, tolerance;
to a friend, your heart;
to your child, a good example;
to a father, deference;
to your mother, conduct that will make her proud of you;
to yourself, respect;
to all men, charity.
John Balfour

When the song of the angels is stilled
When the star in the sky is gone,
When the kings and the princes are home,
When the shepherds are back with their flock,
    The work of Christmas begins:
        To find the lost, to heal the broken,
        To feed the hungry, to release the prisoner,
        To rebuild the nations, to bring peace among brothers,
        To make music in the heart.

Howard Thurman

Yes, if you forgive others their failings, your Heavenly Father will forgive yours, but if you do not forgive others, your Father will not forgive your failings either.

Matt 6:14

Take time to think, it is the source of power.
Take time to read, it is the fountain of wisdom.
Take time to pray, it is the greatest power on earth.
Take time to laugh, it is the music of the soul.
Take time to give, it is too short a day for selfishness.
Take time to love, it is the key to heaven.

Give Me Jesus

When I was a little girl I lived in the city with my father, mother, older brother, and younger brother and sister. We lived on a street of identical houses with brown or green porches and little postage-stamp grass plots in front. We had a little backyard where our flowers grew. Down the corner was a park which surrounded a train station where there were benches, walkways, and a water fountain. We were sheltered by our parents and were not allowed to wander far from our front door. Usually in the summer we sat on our porch and played with paper dolls, painted, or roller-skated. Sometimes we would walk to the avenue with our mother. We were good little children and as I remember it always did as we were told, until...

The summer after I was ten years old, my mother took sick and had a long stay in the hospital. We did not always have a housekeeper to take care of us and since we were eleven, ten, seven, and four — and very responsible — my father, who worked nearby, would sometimes let us take care of ourselves while he would come home at lunch time to check on us.

This worked fine. We all had our chores to do and rules to follow. However, one sunny day, my adventurous spirit took over. I said to my brother, "Let's go on a picnic." We packed the lunch and took my little brother and sister by hand and set off. We had considered going to the park down the corner, but the thought of a magical amusement park about ten miles away lured us. We had been there with our parents and had learned the joy of riding the ferris wheel, the carousel, and the caterpillar. We knew it would be a great place for a picnic! "Don't worry," I assured my brother, "I know the way!" It was a very long walk. We had to cross dangerous streets, a bridge, and wooded land, but we made it! Our bologna sandwiches tasted delicious in the shadow of the great park.

The walk home was harder—the sun was very hot and my little sister complained that she was tired. My brother had to carry her. Finally, bedraggled, sweaty, and weary we arrived home. To our shock, our dad met us on the sidewalk. "Where have you been?" he asked. "I have been searching for you for hours!" It was obvious to us that he was very distraught.

It was only then that I realized what trouble we had caused. Our dad had searched and searched. He had asked neighbors. He had made phone calls. He had no idea where we were. He looked at us in disbelief when we told our tale, but he took us in his arms and forgave us. We knew he loved us in spite of the grief we had caused him.

If

If you can keep your head when all about you
Are losing theirs and blaming it on you;
If you can trust yourself when all men doubt you,
But make allowance for their doubting too;
If you can wait and not be tired by waiting,
Or being lied about, don't deal in lies,
Or being hated don't give way to hating,
And yet don't look too good, nor talk too wise;

If you can dream — and not make dreams your master;
If you can think — and not make thoughts your aim,
If you can meet with Triumph and Disaster
And treat those two Impostors just the same;
If you can bear to hear the truth you've spoken
Twisted by knaves to make a trap for fools,
Or watch the things you gave your life to, broken
And stoop and build 'em up with worn-out tools;

If you can make one heap of all your winnings
And risk it on one turn of pitch-and-toss,
And lose, and start again at your beginnings
And never breathe a word about your loss;
If you can force your heart and nerve and sinew
To serve your turn long after they are gone,
And so hold on when there is nothing in you
Except the Will which says to them: "Hold on!"

If you can talk with crowds and keep your virtue,
Or walk with Kings — nor lose the common touch,
If neither foes nor loving friends can hurt you,
If all men count with you, but none too much;
If you can fill the unforgiving minute
With sixty seconds' worth of distance run,
Yours is the Earth and everything that's in it,
And — which is more — you'll be a Man, my son!

Rudyard Kipling

Troubles are often the tools by which God fashions us for better things.
Henry Ward Beecher

If I cannot do great things, I can do small things in a great way.
James Freeman Clark

And now here is my secret, a very simple secret:
it is only with the heart that one can see rightly,
what is essential is invisible to the eye.
Antoine de Saint-Exupery

We who lived in the concentration camps can remember the men who walked through the huts comforting others, giving away their last piece of bread. They may have been few in number, but they offer sufficient proof that everything can be taken away from a man but one thing: the last of his freedom — to choose one's attitude in any given set of circumstances, to choose one's own way.

Victor E. Frankl

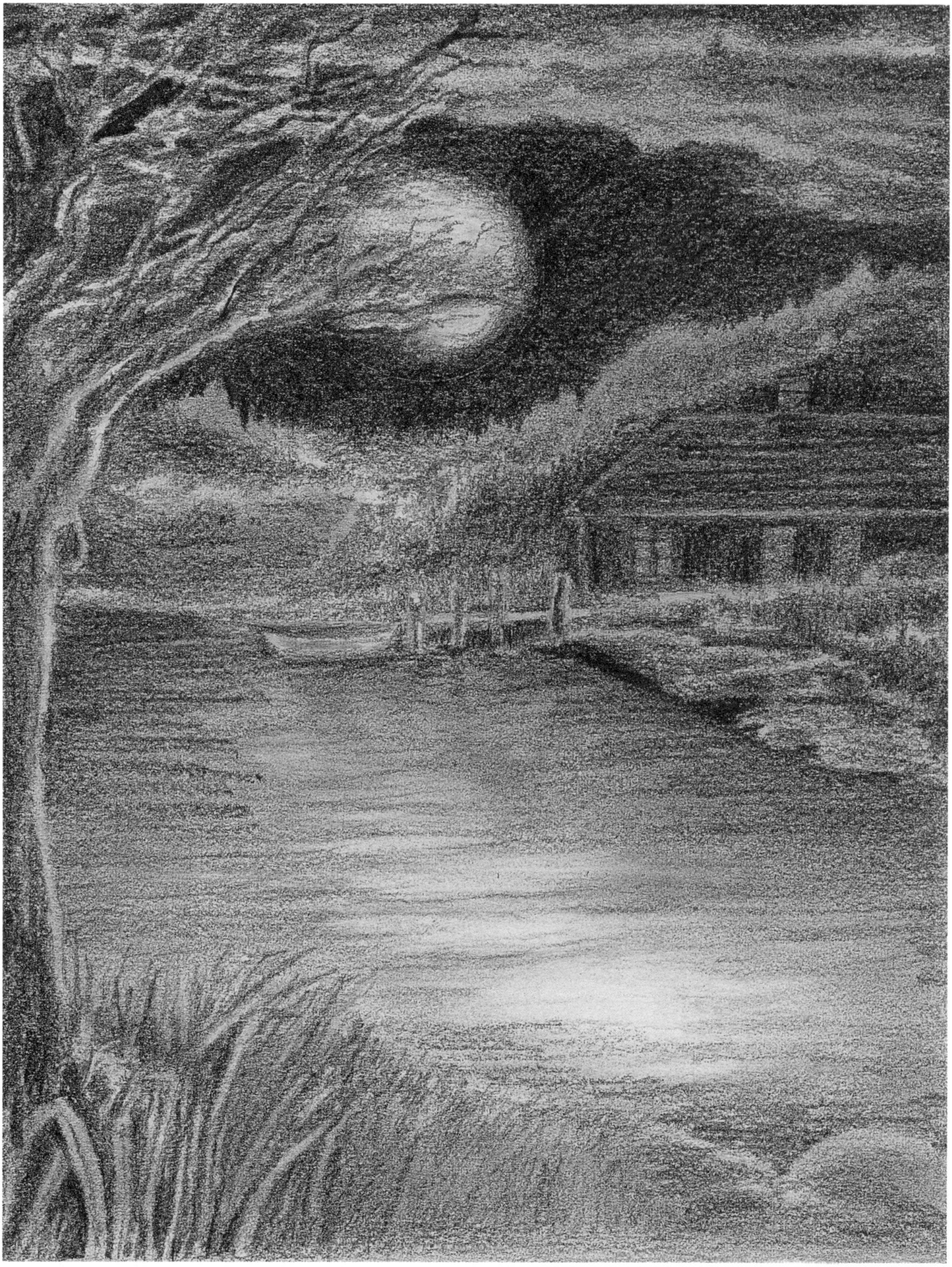

*In the darkness of the night...
Give me Jesus*

Give Me Jesus

Before I lay my head to rest, I hope, for God, I did my best
To say my prayers and help a friend,
From morning time to the day's end.
For God made me and He's proud, I'm sure
Because my thoughts and acts were pure.

Make a rule, and pray God helps you to keep it, never, if possible, lie down at night without being able to say, "I have made one human being, at least, a little wiser, a little happier, or a little better this day."
Charles Kingsley

There are four corners on my bed
Four little angels on my spread
Matthew, Mark, Luke, and John.
God bless the bed I lay upon.
If any evil should come to me.
Please, Lord, awaken me.
Awaken now, awaken, never
I give my soul to God forever.

Now I lay me down to sleep. I pray the Lord my soul to keep. If I should die before I wake, I pray the Lord my soul to take. If I should live for other days, I pray thee, Lord, to guide my ways.

Good night, sweet Jesus, guard us in sleep.
Our souls and bodies in Thy love keep.
Waking or sleeping, keep us in sight.
Dear Gentle Savior, good night, good night.

Give Me Jesus

"Mama, Mama, come quick!" The mother was sure that she heard those words, loud and clear. They seemed to be coming from the direction of her baby's room. She ran to check on her sleeping infant. Just as she expected the little pink bundle was fast asleep. She hadn't moved from the position her mother had placed her ten minutes earlier.

As the mother returned to the living room, she was again startled by the urgent call, "Mama, Mama, come quick!" Although the baby could never have uttered that frantic call, the young mother dashed to the nursery. Again, the baby was just as she had been moments before. A half hour passed and the call came again, this time with a frantic and commanding tone. "Mama, Mama, Mama... come quick!"

Although Mama knew it was not possible for a three month old baby to call her name, she could not resist the call for help, no matter how implausible the situation seemed. She dropped what she was doing and ran to the room. She became weak with fear when she saw that the drapery cord was wrapped around her baby's neck. How had she missed it earlier? The infant was turning blue! The long cord that hung to adjust the curtains had somehow managed to blow into the crib as the baby slept.

The baby's life was saved because the mother reached her just in time. Who called the mother so frantically? Only God knows for sure, but the baby's mother was convinced that it was the child's guardian angel! She repeated the words, "Angel of God, my guardian dear..." As she blessed herself, she vowed that she would say that prayer every morning and night of her life and she did. The lady who told me this story was ninety-two years old and she never forgot her promise — or her angel.

Patricia Gallagher

Watch you, O Lord, those who wake or weep tonight.
Give your angels charge over those who sleep.
Tend your sick ones, rest your weary ones
Bless your dying ones
Smooth your joyous ones. Amen.

Give Me Jesus

Night is falling, dear Mother
The long day is o'er
and before thy loving image
I am kneeling once more
To thank you for keeping me safe through the day
and to ask you this night to
keep the evil one away. Amen

You are richer tonight than you were this morning, if you have taken time to trace the handiwork of God in the commonplace things of life, or if you have been a little blinder to the faults of friend or foe. You are richer if a little child has smiled at you, and a stray dog has licked your hand, or if you have looked for the best in others, and have given others the best in you.

God, make my life a little light,
    Within the world to glow;
A tiny flame that burneth bright
    Wherever I may go.

God, make my life a little flower,
    That giveth joy to all,
Content to bloom in native bower,
    Although its place be small.

God, make my life a little song,
    That comforteth the sad;
That helpeth others to be strong,
    And makes the singer glad.

God, make my life a little staff,
    Whereon the weak may rest,
That so what health and strength I have
May serve my neighbors best.
                        M. Bentham-Edwards

He Who Feeds the Sparrow

He who feeds the sparrow
and guides the robin's flight,
Will raise the sun tomorrow
and light the stars tonight.

His love for us is endless;
His hand can calm the sea.
He who feeds the sparrow,
still cares for you and me.

He showers us with blessings
that we might see and learn
Asking only that we listen
and Love Him in return.

He who feeds the sparrow
and guides the robin's flight,
Will guide my path tomorrow
and give me peace tonight.

Clay Harrison

This above all, to thy own self be true,
then it follows, as the night the day,
thou cannot then be false to any man.

Shakespeare

About the Author

CLAIRE JORDAN MOHAN, formerly of King of Prussia and Lansdale, now resides in Chalfont, Pennsylvania with her husband, Robert. Having retired from full-time teaching at Visitation B.V.M. School in Trooper, PA, she spends her time writing, traveling and enjoying her grandchildren. She is a CCD teacher at her parish and a tutor at Graterford Prison. She has had many articles published in magazines and newspapers and has appeared on national radio and television shows, including Mother Angelica Live, the 700 Club and CNBC. On a recent trip to Rome for the Beatification of Blessed Frances Siedliska, Claire Mohan presented a special edition of her book *"A Red Rose for Frania"* to Pope John Paul II. Her recent book *"The Young Life of Pope John Paul II"* was also hand-delivered to Our Holy Father.

She is the mother of five children and grandmother of twelve. Claire is a graduate of Little Flower High School and is a 1984 summa cum laude graduate of Villanova University where she was valedictorian of her class. She attended Chestnut Hill College for graduate studies. Claire Jordan Mohan welcomes interviews and speaking engagements.

About the Illustrator

JANE ROBBINS' clean, sharp illustrations reflect her classical training. An art major in high school, she was awarded a scholarship to Moore College of Art. She studied at Philadelphia College of Art, and Fleisher's Memorial in Philadelphia, Baum School in Allentown, and Bishop University in Quebec. She taught painting at the YWCA in Philadelphia and has held private art classes in her home.

In addition to Claire Mohan's current book, Mrs. Robbins illustrated Mrs. Mohan's previous books, *"The Young Life of Pope John Paul II"* and *"The Young Life of Mother Teresa of Calcutta"* as well as *"Redheads."* Also, she has written and illustrated articles for magazines. The winner of numerous awards, her work is in private collections throughout the United States and Canada.

Other Books
by Claire Jordan Mohan

A Red Rose for Frania
This children's book offers young readers a thoughtful endearing story of Frances Siedliska's joys and struggles on her pathway to sainthood. This story demonstrates courage and perseverance as it describes Frania's poor health and obstacles in committing to religious life.

Kaze's True Home
This delightful story of the young life of Maria Kaupas will inspire each child as young Casimira follows her star to attain "the impossible dream." "Kaze" as she was called, was neither wealthy nor did she enjoy the opportunities of the young people of today, but she loved God and was able to share her love with others.

The Young Life of Pope John Paul II
Young and old will enjoy this story which details the young life of Pope John Paul II while a boy in Poland. The way Karol Wojtyla handles the triumphs of his life will inspire children to emulate this courageous boy. They learn his life was just like theirs — a mixture of sadness and joy. They meet "a real boy" who shares their hobbies and interests and in the end, grows up to be a most respected religious and world leader.

The Young Life of Mother Teresa of Calcutta
How Gonxha Agnes Bojaxhiu grew to be a world famous personage and a living example of Jesus in a dark world is the basis for this new book for young and old to treasure. This story gives insight into the people and events in Mother Teresa's young life that shaped the final woman — the early death of her beloved father, Nikola, a political figure in the days of unrest of Yugoslavia; — her mother, the warm hospitable Dronda, who always had time for others. We learn how a "pretty mischievous young tomboy" eventually became a world revered "living saint."

Young Sparrow Press • Box 265 • Worcester, PA 19490 • (215) 997-0791

Give Me Jesus

What Others Are Saying...

About... Kaze's True Home

"We live in an era rampant with violence, hate, and fear where the media gives the impression that everyone is corrupt and evil. It is very refreshing to read a story about a contemporary who is a real live saint. A ray of sunshine in a dark world! A marvelous job!" — *Peter A. Mankas, Director, Lansdale Public Library, Lansdale, PA*

"I enjoyed reading the book. I found it interesting, and exciting to follow Casimira on her journeys' — though it also made me cry." — *Rachel Galie, Visitation BVM School, Trooper, PA*

About... The Young Life of Pope John Paul II

"...a delightful read for children... leads the reader into the very soul of that deeply introspective and brilliant young man." — *Catholic Library Association*

"...this is a splendid little book. Children will enjoy it at home and from the school library." — *The Upper Peninsula Catholic*

About... The Young Life of Mother Teresa of Calcutta

"...not only a pleasant introduction to Mother Teresa... but also an inspiring introduction to the life and works of all missionaries... The love and compassion shown in Mother Teresa's quotation will strengthen everyone who reads them." —*Catholic Library Association*

"Here is a loverly book written for children about Mother Teresa... packed with beautiful images to provoke our imagination." — *T.O.R.C.H. Book Reviews*

About... Give Me Jesus

"I really like this book." — *Heather Hinkle, Twin Oaks Elementary School*

"This collection is broad and embracing, touching a variety of inner worlds. It is colorful, playful, intimate, and expressive... As an editor, I find this work delightful." — *Kass Dotterweich, Liguori Publications*

"This book of prayers for children is very inspiring. It presents poems for enjoyment and memorization — a delight!" — *Theresa Johnson, Catholic Heritage Curricula*